Music Genres

R&B and Soul

by C. M. Davis

AF599407

www.focusreaders.com

Copyright © 2025 by Focus Readers®, Mendota Heights, MN 55120. All rights reserved. No part of this book may be reproduced or utilized in any form or by any means without written permission from the publisher.

Focus Readers is distributed by North Star Editions:
sales@northstareditions.com | 888-417-0195

Produced for Focus Readers by Red Line Editorial.

Photographs ©: Casey Flanigan/imageSPACE/Sipa USA/AP Images, cover, 1; Gilles Petard/Redferns/Getty Images, 4, 18; Shutterstock Images, 6, 8, 22, 25, 26, 29; House Of Fame LLC/Michael Ochs Archives/Getty Images, 11; Mark Kettenhofen/Wikimedia Commons, 12; Peter Sekear/Library of Congress, 14; Michael Ochs Archives/Getty Images, 17; Ross Marino/Icon and Image/Michael Ochs Archives/Getty Images, 20–21

Library of Congress Cataloging-in-Publication Data
Names: Davis, C. M. (Children's author) author.
Title: R&B and soul / by C. M. Davis.
Other titles: Rhythm and blues and soul
Description: Mendota Heights, MN: Focus Readers, 2025. | Series: Music genres | Includes index. | Audience: Grades 2-3
Identifiers: LCCN 2024001540 (print) | LCCN 2024001541 (ebook) | ISBN 9798889982050 (hardcover) | ISBN 9798889982616 (paperback) | ISBN 9798889983699 (pdf) | ISBN 9798889983170 (ebook)
Subjects: LCSH: Rhythm and blues music--History and criticism--Juvenile literature. | Soul (Music)--History and criticism--Juvenile literature. | African Americans--Music--History and criticism--Juvenile literature.
Classification: LCC ML3521 .D357 2025 (print) | LCC ML3521 (ebook) | DDC 781.64409--dc23/eng/20240116
LC record available at https://lccn.loc.gov/2024001540
LC ebook record available at https://lccn.loc.gov/2024001541

Printed in the United States of America
Mankato, MN
082024

About the Author

C. M. Davis is a librarian and educator. When she's not reading or writing, she enjoys birdwatching, visiting museums, and hunting for vintage treasures in thrift stores.

Table of Contents

Chapter 1

The Show Begins

It is 1955. A crowd enters the Apollo Theater. The **auditorium** is beautiful. Gold designs decorate the walls. Audience members sit in red velvet seats. They can't wait for the show to start.

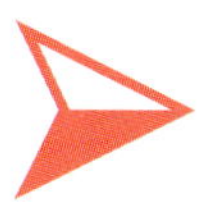

James Brown sang at the Apollo Theater more than 200 times in his career.

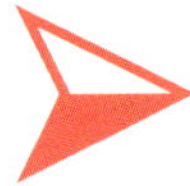

In the 2020s, the Apollo Theater was still hosting shows.

The lights dim, and a velvet curtain rises. The first performers appear on stage. The men in the group wear matching gray suits. They stand in a line. Then the lead singer starts to sing. The other members **harmonize** with him. The lead singer holds his hand over his heart. He feels the lyrics deeply. The **melody** soars.

When the group is done, the crowd claps and cheers. People are excited to hear the next artist.

The Apollo Theater began hosting Amateur Night in the 1930s. The show helped launch many successful artists.

Chapter 2

What Are R&B and Soul?

R&B stands for *rhythm and blues*. The **genre** grew from many different kinds of Black American music. Jazz and blues music influenced R&B. So did swing and folk music.

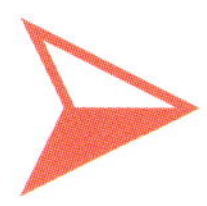

Masego often plays saxophone in his songs. The instrument is common in R&B, soul, and jazz music.

Many R&B songs have strong beats. That helps build a groove. The rhythm makes people want to dance. Bass guitar and drums help create the rhythm. R&B music often includes electric guitar and piano, too.

Vocals are the most important part of R&B. Singers need smooth and powerful voices. They sing beautiful melodies. The best R&B singers show emotion in their performances. Artists such as Otis

Etta James sang songs in several genres. “At Last” from 1960 was one of her biggest hits.

Redding and Etta James did that. They were famous for their voices.

Harmony is important in R&B. Singers add notes above or below the melody to create a nice sound.

Singers such as Whitney Houston got their start singing gospel music.

Many R&B artists are groups. Group members often sing in harmony. Their voices blend together.

Soul music is a subgenre of R&B. Rhythm and vocals are important in soul. Soul also combines R&B

styles with **gospel** singing. Soul songs usually do not have religious lyrics. However, the vocal styles are similar to church music. Many gospel songs use call-and-response. That's when one musician performs a melody. Then another musician responds. Soul often uses call-and-response, too.

Electronic instruments are often used in modern R&B.

Chapter 3

The History of R&B and Soul

Black Americans created R&B. In the 1910s, the **Great Migration** began. Black jazz and blues musicians moved north. They brought their music to new cities. Genres such as swing grew bigger.

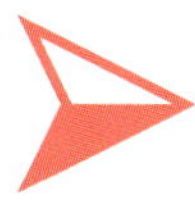

Many Black families moved to big cities such as Memphis, Chicago, and Detroit.

Then artists began mixing all those genres together. By the 1940s, a new style had developed. It was called R&B.

In the 1940s and 1950s, some groups started singing doo-wop. Doo-wop was a kind of R&B. Lyrics included nonsense words and sounds. The Drifters were one of the biggest doo-wop groups. They released many hit songs.

In the early 1950s, **rock and roll** became popular. People saw the

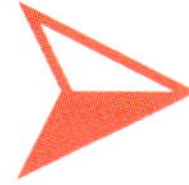

Little Richard was known for his energetic performances.

genre as part of R&B. Fats Domino and Little Richard were stars. By the late 1950s, ways of talking about music had changed. "Rock and roll" was used for white artists. Black artists were called "R&B" instead.

Marvin Gaye had several big hits in the 1960s and 1970s. He is sometimes called the Prince of Soul.

Black musicians developed soul in the late 1950s and early 1960s. The artist James Brown played a key role. People called him the Godfather of Soul. The Motown record label helped spread soul's popularity, too. Motown started famous groups such as the Supremes and the Jackson 5.

In the 1960s and 1970s, more artists found fame. Stevie Wonder and Patti LaBelle became huge stars. So did Gladys Knight and Smokey Robinson.

Some soul artists mixed church music and African rhythms. That led to new genres such as funk and disco.

ARTIST SPOTLIGHT

Aretha Franklin

Aretha Franklin was born in Memphis, Tennessee, in 1942. When she was young, she sang in her church choir. Her amazing singing gained attention. At just 18 years old, Franklin got a record deal.

Audiences loved Franklin's powerful and emotional voice. She became a star. Songs such as "Respect" in 1967 and "(You Make Me Feel Like) A Natural Woman" in 1968 were huge hits. Franklin won 18 Grammy Awards. Music fans remember her as the Queen of Soul.

Aretha Franklin was the first woman in the Rock and Roll Hall of Fame.

Chapter 4

Modern R&B Music

In the 1980s and 1990s, some R&B artists sang in traditional ways. They used older styles. Anita Baker and Luther Vandross did this. People loved their smooth voices.

Anita Baker won eight Grammy Awards for her music.

Other artists tried new things. They mixed R&B with genres such as pop. Some artists became mainstream pop stars. All around the world, fans listened to Michael Jackson and Janet Jackson. Tina Turner and Whitney Houston were huge stars, too.

Those four artists were **soloists**. But vocal groups remained a big part of R&B. In the 1990s, Boyz II Men released many hits. They became the best-selling R&B group

John Legend was inspired by R&B music from the 1990s. He became famous in the 2000s.

of all time. Girl groups did well, too. For example, TLC topped the Billboard Hot 100 many times.

In the 1990s, many performers started pairing R&B with hip-hop. Artists such as Lauryn Hill helped make that sound more popular.

In 2023, SZA's album *SOS* was one of the best-selling albums in the United States.

Rap artists often appeared on R&B songs. Audiences loved it.

In the 2000s, the sound of R&B kept changing. Songs used less piano and guitar. Electronic keyboards became more common.

Usher, Alicia Keys, and John Legend released popular songs.

By the 2020s, R&B was still huge. It was one of the biggest American genres. Bruno Mars and the Weeknd had high streaming numbers and lots of radio play. In 2023, Beyoncé held a global stadium tour. And R&B soloist SZA topped the charts.

Mariah Carey's music mixed R&B with pop. By 2024, she had 19 No. 1 hits.

FOCUS ON

R&B and Soul

Write your answers on a separate piece of paper.

1. Write a few sentences describing some common features of R&B music.
2. Do you prefer R&B music or soul music? Why?
3. When did R&B music develop as a new genre?
   - A. the 1940s
   - B. the 1980s
   - C. the 2000s
4. Why might R&B artists mix their sounds with other genres?
   - A. Most fans only like one genre.
   - B. Artists and fans often like several genres.
   - C. Making music in one genre is difficult.

5. What does **decorate** mean in this book?

*The auditorium is beautiful. Gold designs **decorate** the walls.*

- **A.** to make something look nice
- **B.** to hide something
- **C.** to make something look bad

6. What does **mainstream** mean in this book?

*Some artists became **mainstream** pop stars. All around the world, fans listened to Michael Jackson and Janet Jackson.*

- **A.** no longer making music
- **B.** known by very few people
- **C.** known by many people

Answer key on page 32.

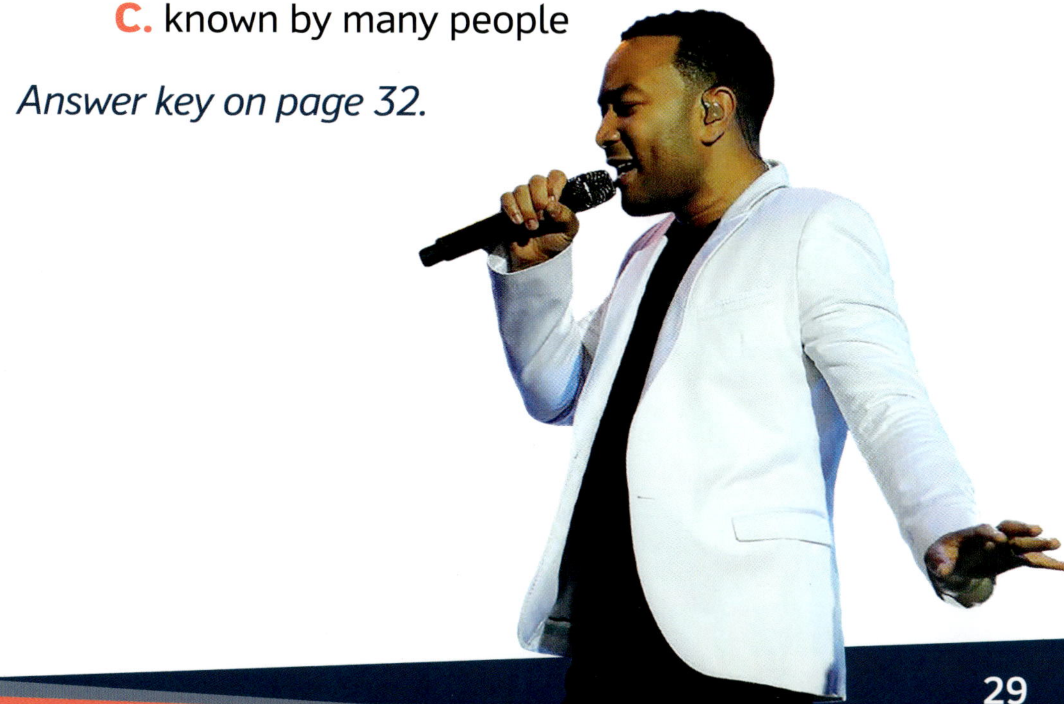

Glossary

amateur
Someone who is not paid to perform an activity.

auditorium
The part of a theater where the audience sits.

genre
A category of music, such as rock, pop, or country.

gospel
A style of Christian music featuring vocal harmonies and religious lyrics.

Great Migration
A movement of six million Black Americans to northern cities from 1910 to 1970.

harmonize
To sing or play notes that blend with a song's melody.

melody
The tune in a piece of music.

rock and roll
A type of dance music with heavy beats and simple melodies.

soloists
People who perform alone, not as part of a group.

vocals
The part of music involving singing.

To Learn More

BOOKS

Felix, Rebecca. *Lizzo: Singing Superstar.* Minneapolis: Abdo Publishing, 2022.

London, Martha. *Bruno Mars*. Mendota Heights, MN: Focus Readers, 2021.

Smith, Elliott. *Black Achievements in Music.* Minneapolis: Lerner Publications, 2024.

NOTE TO EDUCATORS

Visit **www.focusreaders.com** to find lesson plans, activities, links, and other resources related to this title.

Index

Answer Key: 1. Answers will vary; **2.** Answers will vary; **3.** A; **4.** B; **5.** A; **6.** C